A LOOK AT YOUR GOVERNMENT

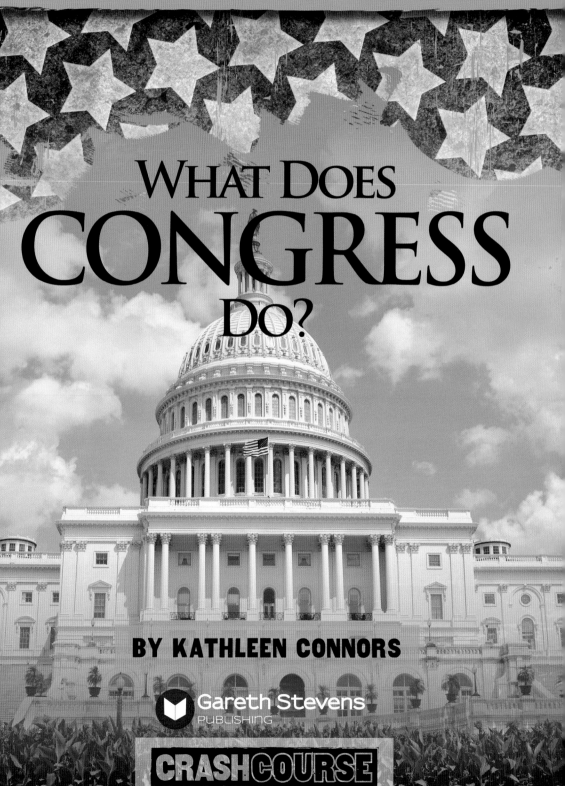

WHAT DOES
CONGRESS
DO?

BY KATHLEEN CONNORS

Gareth Stevens
PUBLISHING

CRASH COURSE

Please visit our website, www.garethstevens.com. For a free color catalog of all our high-quality books, call toll free 1-800-542-2595 or fax 1-877-542-2596.

Cataloging-in-Publication Data

Names: Connors, Kathleen.
Title: What does Congress do? / Kathleen Connors.
Description: New York : Gareth Stevens Publishing, 2018. | Series: A look at your government | Includes index.
Identifiers: ISBN 9781482460476 (pbk.) | ISBN 9781482460490 (library bound) | ISBN 9781482460483 (6 pack)
Subjects: LCSH: United States. Congress--Juvenile literature. | Legislative power--United States--Juvenile literature. | Legislation--United States--Juvenile literature.
Classification: LCC JK1025.C66 2018 | DDC 328.73--dc23

First Edition

Published in 2018 by
Gareth Stevens Publishing
111 East 14th Street, Suite 349
New York, NY 10003

Editor: Kristen Nelson
Designer: Samantha DeMartin

Photo credits: Series art MaxyM/Shutterstock.com; cover, pp. 1, 5 (judicial) Orhan Cam/ Shutterstock.com; p. 5 (legislative) Chris Parypa Photography/Shutterstock.com; p. 5 (executive) Miljan Mladenovic/Shutterstock.com; pp. 7, 25 Drop of Light/Shutterstock.com; p. 9 Win McNamee/Getty Images News/Getty Images; p. 11 Joseph Sohm/Shutterstock.com; p. 13 Chip Somodevilla/Getty Images News/Getty Images; p. 15 Christopher Halloran/Shutterstock.com; p. 17 Joseph Sohm/Shutterstock.com; pp. 19, 23 Bill Clark/CQ-Roll Call Group/Getty Images; p. 21 Lyubov Timofeyeva/Shutterstock.com; p. 27 (both) Brendan Hoffman/Getty Images News/Getty Images; p. 29 Crush Rush/Shutterstock.com; p. 30 (capitol icon) vector toon/ Shutterstock.com.

Printed in the United States of America

CPSIA compliance information: Batch #CS17GS: For further information contact Gareth Stevens, New York, New York at 1-800-542-2595.

CONTENTS

Words in the glossary appear in **bold** type the first time they are used in the text.

THREE BRANCHES

The government of the United States is made up of three branches. Congress is the legislative, or lawmaking, branch. The US **Constitution** divides Congress into two parts, or houses: the Senate and the House of **Representatives**.

MAKE THE GRADE

The president heads the **executive** branch of the US government. The highest court in the United States, the Supreme Court, heads the **judicial** branch.

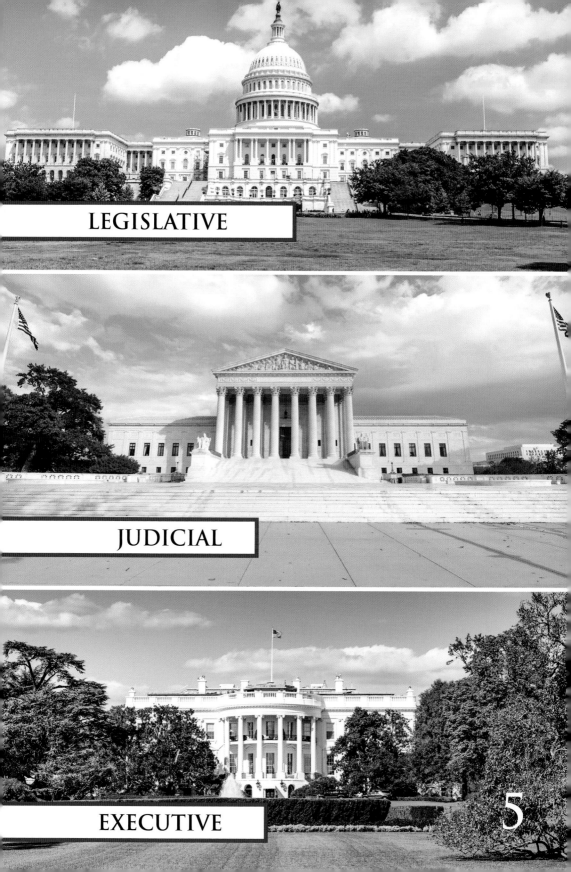

LEGISLATIVE

JUDICIAL

EXECUTIVE

5

All About the Senate

The Senate has 100 members. Two senators are **elected** from each state. The Senate is the smaller house, so each senator's vote has great importance. Senators serve 6-year terms, or periods in office.

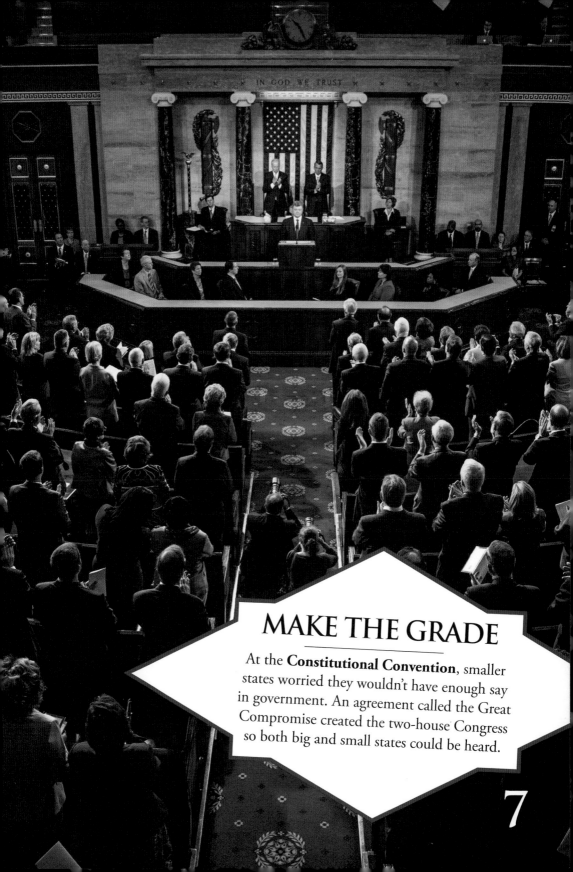

MAKE THE GRADE

At the **Constitutional Convention**, smaller states worried they wouldn't have enough say in government. An agreement called the Great Compromise created the two-house Congress so both big and small states could be heard.

To serve in Congress, senators must be at least 30 years old, have been a US **citizen** for at least 9 years, and live in the state they represent. Senators are elected directly by votes cast by people in their state.

MAKE THE GRADE

Every even-numbered year, there's an election for about one-third of the seats in the Senate.

Senators have long terms to allow them time to work on big problems. They can consider laws' lasting effects. Senators have no term limit, which means they can keep getting reelected. This may give them lots of time for their **agenda**.

MAKE THE GRADE

The vice president of the United States is the head of the Senate. If there's ever a tie vote, the vice president casts the deciding vote.

VICE PRESIDENT AL GORE

INSIDE THE HOUSE

The House of Representatives has 435 members. The number of representatives each state has in the House is based on state population. States are divided into areas called congressional districts. Each district elects a representative to serve in the House.

MAKE THE GRADE

As part of the Great Compromise, the House of Representatives was created to give states with larger populations more say in one house of Congress.

13

To be elected to the House, representatives must be at least 25 years old, have been a US citizen for at least 7 years, and live in the state they want to represent. House representatives serve 2-year terms.

MAKE THE GRADE

The Speaker of the House leads the House of Representatives. The members of the House elect the Speaker to a 2-year term.

SPEAKER OF THE HOUSE
PAUL RYAN

15

The Founding Fathers gave House representatives a short term for a reason. They wanted to **encourage** House representatives to meet their district's needs quickly. They thought the representatives might lose touch with people's needs if they were in Congress too long.

MAKE THE GRADE

Members of Congress are commonly members of the two main political parties, the Democrats and the Republicans. They don't have to be, though!

CONGRESSMAN
JOHN LEWIS

17

WORKING TOGETHER

Once elected, members of both the Senate and the House of Representatives work on committees, or small groups, within their house. Each committee **focuses** on one area of government. Those on the committee are often very knowledgeable in that area.

MAKE THE GRADE

Some congressional committees focus on schools, farming, and how the United States deals with other countries.

Rep. Debbie Dingell

The houses of Congress work together to make laws. Either house can introduce, or first present, a bill. Committees work on it before the whole House or Senate sees it. Both houses have to pass a bill before the president sees it.

MAKE THE GRADE

Only the House of Representatives can introduce a bill that raises revenue, or money, for the US government.

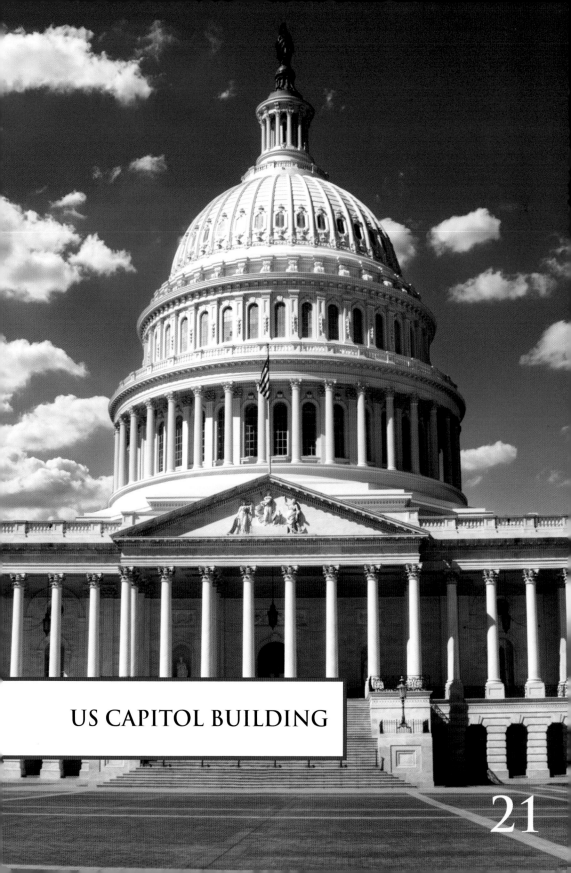

US CAPITOL BUILDING

21

In addition to making laws, Congress has other powers given by the US Constitution. It can collect taxes, create money for citizens to use, and **declare** war. The Constitution says Congress can't do some things, too, such as crown a king!

MAKE THE GRADE

The Constitution states that Congress can make any laws it feels are "necessary and proper," or fitting, for the government to run.

SENATOR
CHARLES SCHUMER

23

CHECKS AND BALANCES

The president balances the power of Congress by using a veto, which stops bills from becoming law. The Supreme Court makes sure laws are faithful to the Constitution.

MAKE THE GRADE

The Senate is able to check and balance the president by voting on the people the president chooses for certain offices, including the Supreme Court.

AMENDING THE CONSTITUTION

Congress may **propose** amendments, or changes, to the Constitution. Two-thirds of both houses of Congress must vote in favor of an amendment proposal for it to pass. This doesn't happen very often.

MAKE THE GRADE

Before an amendment becomes part of the Constitution, three-fourths of states have to ratify, or vote in favor of, it.

26

27

BACK HOME

While much of Congress's work is for the US government, they also represent many people in their state. Senators and House representatives try to make these citizens' voices heard. They work to make life in their state better.

MAKE THE GRADE

Members of Congress spend a lot of time in Washington, DC, making laws. They also spend time in their home state listening to citizens there.

SENATOR
BERNIE SANDERS

29

MEMBERS OF
CONGRESS

	HOUSE OF REPRESENTATIVES	SENATE
age	must be 25 or older	must be 30 or older
length of citizenship	at least 7 years	at least 9 years
length of term	2 years	6 years
number of members	435	100
number of representatives from each state	depends on population	2

GLOSSARY

agenda: things someone wants to get done or talk about

citizen: someone who lives in a country legally and has certain rights

constitution: the basic laws by which a country or state is governed

Constitutional Convention: a meeting that took place in 1787 to address problems in the original US constitution

declare: to make an official announcement

elect: to choose for a position in a government

encourage: to try to get to do something

executive: having to do with the carrying out of the law

focus: to direct attention

judicial: having to do with the courts

propose: to offer for consideration

representative: a member of a lawmaking body who represents, or acts for, voters

FOR MORE INFORMATION

BOOKS

McAuliffe, Bill. *The U.S. Senate*. Mankato, MN: Creative Education, 2016.

Rose, Simon. *The House of Representatives*. New York, NY: AV2 by Weigl, 2015.

WEBSITES

Congress for Kids

congressforkids.net

Learn much more about Congress and how the US government works!

Publisher's note to educators and parents: Our editors have carefully reviewed these websites to ensure that they are suitable for students. Many websites change frequently, however, and we cannot guarantee that a site's future contents will continue to meet our high standards of quality and educational value. Be advised that students should be closely supervised whenever they access the Internet.

INDEX